LGBTQ Without Borders
INTERNATIONAL LIFE

BONAPART

Beyond Male and Female: The Gender Identity Spectrum

Body and Mind: LGBTQ Health Issues

Double Challenge: Being LGBTQ and a Minority

Gender Fulfilled: Being Transgender

LGBTQ Without Borders: International Life

LGBTQ at Work: Your Personal and Working Life

Love Makes a Family: Friends, Family, and Significant Others

When You're Ready: Coming Out

You Are Not Alone: Finding Your LGBTQ Community

LGBTQ WITHOUT BORDERS
INTERNATIONAL LIFE

By Jeremy Quist

Mason Crest
Philadelphia • Miami

Mason Crest
450 Parkway Drive, Suite D
Broomall, PA 19008
(866) MCP-BOOK (toll free)
www.masoncrest.com

First printing
9 8 7 6 5 4 3 2 1
Series ISBN: 978-1-4222-4273-5
Hardcover ISBN: 978-1-4222-4279-7
E-book ISBN: 978-1-4222-7526-9

Cataloging-in-Publication Data is available on file at the Library of Congress.

Developed and Produced by Print Matters Productions, Inc. (www.printmattersinc.com)

Cover and Interior Design by Tim Palin Creative

QR CODES AND LINKS TO THIRD-PARTY CONTENT

CONTENTS

Foreword 6

Introduction 8

1   Latin America and Europe 14

2   Middle East and Africa 30

3   Asia and Oceania 44

4   International LGBTQ Issues 60

5   International Relations 74

Series Glossary of Key Terms 90

Further Reading & Internet Resources. 93

Index 95

Author's Biography & Credits 96

KEY ICONS TO LOOK FOR

WORDS TO UNDERSTAND: These words, with their easy-to-understand definitions, will increase readers' understanding of the text while building vocabulary skills.

SIDEBARS: This boxed material within the main text allows readers to build knowledge, gain insights, explore possibilities, and broaden their perspectives by weaving together additional information to provide realistic and holistic perspectives.

EDUCATIONAL VIDEOS: Readers can view videos by scanning our QR codes, providing them with additional educational content to supplement the text.

TEXT-DEPENDENT QUESTIONS: These questions send the reader back to the text for more careful attention to the evidence presented there.

RESEARCH PROJECTS: Readers are pointed toward areas of further inquiry connected to each chapter. Suggestions are provided for projects that encourage deeper research and analysis.

SERIES GLOSSARY OF KEY TERMS: This back-of-the-book glossary contains terminology used throughout this series. Words found here increase the reader's ability to read and comprehend higher-level books and articles in this field.

I'm so excited that you've decided to pick up this book! I can't tell you how much something like this would have meant to me when I was in high school in the early 2000s. Thinking back on that time, I can honestly say I don't recall ever reading anything positive about the LGBTQ community. And while *Will & Grace* was one of the most popular shows on television at the time, it never made me feel as though such stories could be a reality for me. That's in part why it took me nearly a decade more to finally come out in 2012 when I was 25 years old; I guess I knew so little about what it meant to be LGBTQ that I was never really able to come to terms with the fact that I was queer myself.

But times have changed so much since then. In the United States alone, marriage equality is now the law of the land; conversion therapy has been banned in more than 15 states (and counting!); all 50 states have been served by an openly LGBTQ-elected politician in some capacity at some time; and more LGBTQ artists and stories are being celebrated in music, film, and on television than ever before. And that's just the beginning! It's simply undeniable: *it gets better.*

After coming out and becoming the proud queer person I am today, I've made it my life's goal to help share information that lets others know that they're never alone. That's why I now work for the It Gets Better Project (www.itgetsbetter.org), a nonprofit with a mission to uplift, empower, and connect LGBTQ youth around the globe. The organization was founded in September 2010 when the first It Gets Better video was uploaded to YouTube. The viral online storytelling movement that quickly followed has generated over 60,000 video stories to date, one of the largest collections of LGBTQ stories the world has ever seen.

Since then, the It Gets Better Project has expanded into a global organization, working to tell stories and build communities everywhere. It does this through three core programs:

- **Media.** We continue to expand our story collection to reflect the vast diversity of the global LGBTQ community and to make it ever more accessible to LGBTQ youth everywhere. (See, itgetsbetter.org/stories.)
- **Global.** Through a growing network of affiliates, the It Gets Better Project is helping to equip communities with the knowledge, skills, and resources they need to tell their own stories. (See, itgetsbetter.org/global.)
- **Education.** It Gets Better stories have the power to inform our communities and inspire LGBTQ allies, which is why we're working to share them in as many classrooms and community spaces we can. (See, itgetsbetter.org/education.)

You can help the It Gets Better Project make a difference in the lives of LGBTQ young people everywhere. To get started, go to www.itgetsbetter.org and click "Get Involved." You can also help by sharing this book and the other incredible volumes from the LGBTQ Life series with someone you know and care about. You can also share them with a teacher or community leader, who will in turn share them with countless others. That's how movements get started.

In short, I'm so proud to play a role in helping to bring such an important collection like this to someone like you. I hope you enjoy each and every book, and please don't forget: *it gets better.*

Justin Tindall
Director, Education and
Global Programming
It Gets Better Project

INTRODUCTION

There are approximately 7.5 billion people in the world. The percentage of people who are LGBTQ is extremely difficult to pin down, but estimates based on research range from 3 to 10 percent, which means that there are somewhere between 225 million and 750 million LGBTQ people in the world. That represents hundreds of millions of different life experiences, hundreds of different cultures and ethnicities, and 195 different countries. The breadth of experience within the community we call LGBTQ is difficult to even imagine.

A WEALTH OF DIVERSITY

The purpose of this book is to help you understand the incredible diversity of LGBTQ people around the world. With that in mind, there's an important principle you should remember while you're studying LBGTQ communities in foreign countries: LGBTQ doesn't look the same in every cultural context. When we use words to describe sexual and gender minorities—lesbian, gay, bisexual, transgender, queer, pansexual, asexual, genderqueer, and many others—we are using those words to try to understand very complex issues. None of those terms is a perfect description of what is going on inside a person, but they're the tools we use to communicate these identities as well as we possibly can. Our own culture has changed the way we talk about and perceive identity over time, so it shouldn't be surprising that different cultures have different ways of talking about sexual and gender identity and even have different conceptions of what queerness looks like.

The LGBTQ *communities* in different areas can look different as well. There are certain things that we take for granted as parts of the community, such as pride parades, rainbow flags, and gay bars. But we can't assume that that's how it will look everywhere. Those things grew out of a very specific time and context, and situations that didn't happen exactly the same way in other places. For example, the first pride parade took place to mark the first anniversary of the Stonewall Riots in New York City; it was meant to fill a specific purpose in a specific place. The rainbow flag was not a symbol for the community until the 1970s, starting in San Francisco. Although LGBTQ people around the world have adopted many of these symbols, not necessarily every culture has done so.

Often when people talk about LGBTQ rights in another country, they talk about whether pride parades and gay businesses exist, as well as the status of same-sex relationships, as the measure of a society's acceptance—for example, marriage or civil unions. Although these laws are important and can provide clues as to the quality of life for LGBTQ people, they are not the only things to consider.

Take the example of the Czech Republic, in Central Europe, which is considered one of the most liberal countries, even within Europe. Despite this openness, the country did not recognize gay relationships legally until 2006, didn't hold its first pride parade until 2011, and still hasn't legalized gay marriage, which seems completely out of order if you're measuring in terms of how things have progressed in some other Western countries. Different societies have different priorities and different ways of progressing, and that's usually okay.

The more limited way of measuring a country's openness also ignores the situation for transgender people. Same-sex marriage being legal doesn't necessarily help gender minorities if they are unable to live their lives in peace while being their authentic selves.

A society, country, or culture cannot be measured on a clear scale between "accepting" and "not accepting." It's more complicated than that, and we should be sensitive to that as we study other cultures.

AN IMPORTANT PATTERN

As you read the following chapters about different places in the world, you'll notice how rich the diversity of peoples and cultures is.

You'll also notice, however, that some patterns emerge. One of the most prevalent patterns that emerges is the impact that European colonization of areas across the planet had upon the world's attitudes toward LGBTQ people. From the 1400s through the 1900s, European countries conquered and settled in areas all around the world. Sometimes they did this to make trade more possible with those regions, bringing home greater wealth. Sometimes it was just for the land itself. Sometimes it was for the prestige of ruling as many people as possible. The British were fond of saying that "the sun never sets on the British Empire," meaning that they ruled so many different areas of the world that the sun was always shining on land they controlled.

But the European powers were not satisfied in just ruling people all over the world. Because the Christian nations believed that people who were not Christian were doomed to eternal hellfire if they did not convert, they believed they were saving the souls of the people of the world by bringing them their religion. Christianity at the time was especially hostile to LGBTQ people. Much of Britain's colonial period, for example, was within what is called the Victorian Era, an especially conservative period in British history in which very strict social expectations were enforced upon all subjects of the empire.

This imperialism greatly affected perceptions of LGBTQ people all over the world. Wherever the Europeans went, the laws they imposed upon the natives brought them in line with European culture, including laws about LGBTQ people. Laws forbidding male homosexuality were particularly specific, but gender non-conformity was condemned as well.

Unfortunately, this means that a lot of the sexual and gender diversity that existed in these societies was suppressed. Some evidence of what was there is left, but much is lost. We can't know exactly what many of these cultures' attitudes were before colonization—maybe some of them already had a bias against sexual and gender minorities—but we do know that many societies' attitudes were, in fact, shaped by colonization. In addition to the knowledge we have of some cultures' histories, which we will discuss, we can know that diversity existed because, as the human rights advocate Peter Tatchell points out on his Web site, "If there was no homosexuality … why bother to include laws criminalizing it, unless to target those who were practicing it?"

THE LEGACY OF COLONIALISM

Many of the societies that these laws were forced upon have taken them to heart so strongly that they feel that their negative attitudes toward LGBTQ people are part of their native culture, even if their pre-colonial history had no such negativity. They talk about the new pressure on human rights from outside forces as a new kind of imperialism—"cultural imperialism" or "neo-colonialism." And they're not completely wrong. It's one of the deep ironies of history that the European and North American countries that are trying to take the lead on acceptance of LGBTQ people are the same countries that shaped much of the world's negative attitudes in the first place.

This history can make it even more difficult for LGBTQ organizations and individuals in their work to gain LGBTQ rights. Countries that had anti-LGBTQ laws forced upon them now defend those laws against outside pressure that they perceive as trying to meddle in their countries. They double-down on colonial laws to fight against neo-colonialism.

FAR TO GO

According to the International Lesbian, Gay, Bisexual, Trans, and Intersex Association (ILGBTIA), an international advocacy group, 72 out of the 195 countries in the world have laws targeting sexual or gender minorities. The cultures of many other countries make it difficult for

LGBTQ people to live openly and freely. This means that since there are still so many places in the world where LGBTQ people aren't accepted, it's likely that there are hundreds of millions of people still in the closet across the globe. Although as a human race we have come far in learning to accept sexual and gender minorities, we still have so very far to go.

There is an incredible diversity of LGBTQ people around the world.

1

Latin America and Europe

WORDS TO UNDERSTAND

INDIGENOUS: Native to a certain place.

IRON CURTAIN: During the Cold War, the border in Europe between communist and democratic countries.

SUPRANATIONAL: An organization that operates above the level of a national government.

TWO-SPIRIT: A Native American term for LGBTQ people, indicating that they have both male and female aspects.

Latin America refers to the parts of North and South America that were originally conquered and settled by the Spanish and Portuguese. This includes everything from Mexico in North America down to the southern tip of South America.

LATIN AMERICA

The history of Latin America did not begin with the arrival of European colonists, of course, but they were so successful in erasing the **indigenous** culture that it's hard to know what the attitudes of the natives were toward LGBTQ people.

One clue we might have about what it was like for LGBTQ people before the Spanish arrived comes from the remaining indigenous cultures of North America. Many Native American tribes have a history of people who are referred to, in English, as **"two-spirit,"** meaning they have aspects of both male and female in them. Sometimes people use this term narrowly to refer to transgender or non-binary people, but it is also used as a broader term for all LGBTQ people. Some of the history of two-spirit people has been lost but it's believed that they played an important, specific role within many Native American tribes.

Latin America is strongly Catholic, which shapes attitudes toward LGBTQ people.

When the Spanish arrived in what we now consider Latin America, they brought with them their strong religious belief in the Catholic Church. Thus, they established missions to convert the natives—often violently—to Catholicism. Consequently, Latin America is strongly Catholic to this day, which shapes many attitudes toward LGBTQ people. The Catholic Church's position is that sexual identities other than heterosexual and gender identities other than the male/female binary as determined at birth are sinful, so the dominant culture of Latin America has generally agreed with that.

The Direction of LGBTQ Rights in Latin America

The situation has been changing, though. According to Human Rights Watch, an international advocacy organization, "Argentina, Colombia, Brazil, and Uruguay recognize same-sex marriage nationally. Mexico does too, but in two-thirds of its states, same-sex couples must undertake a slow, burdensome, and costly judicial procedure not required of different-sex couples."

In addition, the Inter-American Court of Human Rights, a **supranational** organization that represents all of Latin America, ruled that countries must allow same-sex marriage and allow transgender people to legally change their gender. Although the ruling does not *force* the countries to change their laws, it applies pressure to do so and shows movement in the direction of a more open Latin America.

The culture of Latin America has become more favorable to LGBTQ people.

Even more importantly, the culture of Latin America has become more favorable to LGBTQ people. A *U.S. News* survey reported that "82 percent of people in the Americas, including Latin America, believe LGBT individuals should have the same rights as non-LGBT folks." But obstacles remain. The same study points out the high amount of anti-LGBTQ violence that still occurs in the Americas. And the Catholic Church continues to advocate for a hardline anti-LGBTQ position.

Mexico

Like much of Latin America, Mexico's history is tied closely to the Spanish. But unlike most other countries in the region, Mexico also

The first LGBTQ rights organization in Mexico, called the Homosexual Liberation Front, was founded in 1971.

experienced a six-year period of occupation by France, beginning in 1861. This led to the adoption of the Napoleonic Code, a French system of laws that did not criminalize homosexuality. Although this does not indicate an acceptance of LGBTQ people, it does create a unique situation in which the Catholic Church's rules were not as directly reflected in the law as in other areas of the Spanish sphere of influence.

The first LGBTQ rights organization was founded in 1971, called the Homosexual Liberation Front. Later, Mexico City took the lead in the legal recognition of same-sex relationships, with civil unions being recognized in the city in 2006, and marriage in 2009. Same-sex marriage became legal nationwide in June 2015, following a ruling by Mexico's Supreme Court—the same month the U.S. Supreme Court made a similar ruling.

Brazil was one of the first countries to adopt LGBTQ rights laws.

On a cultural level, many Mexicans still have negative attitudes toward LGBTQ rights, but the change in laws reflects an ongoing shift.

Brazil

Brazil's path is unique within the Americas. Having been colonized by the Portuguese instead of the Spanish, its connection to the Catholic Church is just as strong, but its culture remains distinct from those of the countries around it.

Brazil's attitude toward LGBTQ people is contradictory. The country is famously permissive, with world-famous raucous festivals and party cities lining the coast. São Paolo is also known for hosting the largest pride celebrations in the world. And Brazil was one of the first countries to adopt LGBTQ rights laws. But at the same time, Brazil also has one of the highest rates of violence toward LGBTQ people, with trans women being especially at risk of violence. LGBTQ people in Brazil are in the unfortunate position of having legal protections, while still facing danger in their everyday lives.

A handful of trans-rights organizations in El Salvador fight to pass gender identity laws.

ALDO

Aldo Alexander Peña is a transgender man from El Salvador, in Central America. After he was nearly beaten to death by the police, he became politically active as an advocate for LGBTQ rights in his country, even running for a seat on El Salvador's mayoral council. According to the Web site Quartz, "His current priority—and that of the handful of trans-rights organizations in El Salvador—is passing a gender identity law to allow trans Salvadorans to legally change their name and gender."

"It's not that we don't want to be able to get married and have kids one day," Peña told Quartz. "But when we think about it, if they are already denying us the right to gender identity so profoundly, how will they respond the day that LGBT organizations in El Salvador start to fight for same-sex marriage?"

Europe is generally considered to be the most open region of the world for LGBTQ people.

EUROPE

Europe is generally considered to be the most open region of the world for LGBTQ people. To a large degree, that reputation is earned, but it also should not be overstated. Europe's history provides a very complicated legacy with regard to the treatment of sexual and gender minorities.

The most documented ancient civilizations of Europe—Greece and Rome—are well known to have been more open to same-sex relationships. Most of the historical record is about gay or bisexual male relationships, but there was also a famous female poet named Sappho, who wrote love poems to women. (Her home island of Lesbos became the root of the word *lesbian*.) It wasn't until the Christian period of history that Europeans' attitudes became much more negative toward LGBTQ people. This began in the very early years of the religion, but only accelerated through the Middle Ages, from the 5th to 15th centuries. Homosexuality was considered one of the most serious sins a person could commit, and the punishments for these sins were extreme. When the European powers turned outward and began taking over lands across the world, they brought with them their hostility toward LGBTQ people.

The first-ever gay rights movement in the world was in Germany in the late 19th and early 20th centuries.

A Major Reversal

Despite this history, in modern times, some countries in Europe have led the charge for LGBTQ rights. For example, the Netherlands was the first country in the world to legalize gay marriage in 2001. Cultural attitudes in the United Kingdom, France, the Netherlands, Spain, Norway, and Sweden have been more open to sexual and gender minorities for decades. The first-ever gay rights movement in the world was in Germany in the late 19th and early 20th centuries, although it was unfortunately destroyed by the Nazis before and during World War II.

Although Eastern Europe is no longer communist, some of the attitudes that came out of the Cold War still exist.

Although religion has historically played a very strong role in the culture, in today's Europe the impact of religion on LGBTQ attitudes varies significantly among countries. For example, Spain and Italy are both very strongly Catholic countries, but Spain is one of the most accepting countries in the world, while Italy maintains a more closed position. Ireland, until very recently, was very strongly influenced by its Catholic faith, but that power has been fading over the last few years; Ireland ended up voting to allow same-sex marriage.

Many of the countries of Western Europe are largely irreligious, meaning they don't have strong religious beliefs or don't consider themselves part of a particular religion. This is especially true of countries that are historically Protestant Christian countries. In places such as the Netherlands, Norway, Sweden, and Denmark, it's uncommon to be devoutly religious.

Eastern Europe

When people discuss LGBTQ rights in Europe, they are usually talking about Western Europe. The situation can be very different in Eastern Europe. During the Cold War, which lasted between the end of World War II to around 1989, much of Eastern Europe was behind the **Iron Curtain**. This meant that they were highly influenced by communism and by the Soviet Union. Most communist countries took a hardline stance opposed to LGBTQ people, though it varied a little bit from country to country. Under communism as it existed in most of Europe, a person's worth was based upon their usefulness to society as a whole. A person was expected to be a loyal citizen and a hard worker ... and they were expected to bear and raise good communist children. Anyone who didn't fit into that ideal was considered a threat to the communist order. That included gender and sexual minorities.

Although the countries of Eastern Europe are no longer communist, some of the attitudes that came out of that era still exist. In some countries, that includes an anti-LGBTQ bias. However, there are exceptions. The Czech Republic, which has a communist legacy, is one of the most open and permissive countries in the world.

Some countries of Eastern Europe, like Slovakia and Poland, are now heavily influenced by the Catholic Church and therefore are opposed to LGBTQ rights. Others, like Russia, Romania, and Serbia, are very influenced by the Eastern Orthodox Church, which is just as unaccepting as the Catholic Church. In the Balkan region, the Catholic Church, the Eastern Orthodox Church, and Islam all hold sway over significant portions of society—none of which is friendly to LGBTQ people.

As the largest and most powerful country to emerge from the Soviet Union as it fell apart, Russia's attitudes toward LGBTQ people continue to be shaped by its communist history. The growth of the power of the Orthodox Church has only made matters worse. Russian President Vladimir Putin has a cozy relationship with the church's leadership. He supports their causes, like stifling LGBTQ rights, and they drum up support for him among the church's members. A Russian law criminalizing LGBTQ "propaganda" has been used as an excuse to suppress any public demonstration of homosexuality or gender nonconformity.

Russia is also home to one of the greatest human rights tragedies currently facing LGBTQ people in the world. Chechnya is a majority-Muslim, largely self-governed region of Russia that has been persecuting, arresting, torturing, and in some cases, killing LGBTQ people, particularly gay men. President Putin has purposefully turned a blind eye as the Chechen government commits atrocities. The leader of Chechnya, Ramzan Kadyrov, has denied the reports of human rights organizations and the people who have experienced the persecution, even going so far as to declare that there are no people "like that" in his country. Human rights organizations have been working to help LGBTQ people escape the region, but the situation is ongoing.

Russian law criminalizing LGBTQ "propaganda" has been used to suppress any public demonstration of homosexuality.

Europe is a great example of an area that should not be assumed to have one attitude across all countries. Although its reputation as being on the forefront of LGBTQ rights is earned, that does not reflect the day-to-day life of every LGBTQ person on the continent. Some still face strong opposition from their culture, religion, and government.

The Romanian Orthodox Church, which has a massive amount of power and deep ties to the government, is also extremely anti-LGBTQ.

The European Union and LGBTQ Rights

The European Union is a supranational organization that ties together 28 countries in Europe (27 after the United Kingdom leaves). The countries of the EU have made a series of agreements that set

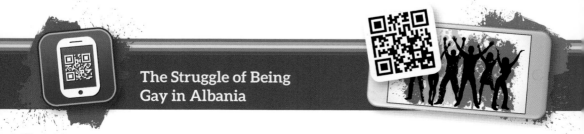

The Struggle of Being Gay in Albania

priorities and common policies across much of the continent. In practice, Western Europe has greater power within the Union because the countries were the founding members of the organization, especially France, Germany, and Belgium.

For LGBTQ people, this means that countries that are open to LGBTQ people have some power to support them in Eastern European countries

The European Union actively supports LGBTQ organizations throughout Europe.

Tiberiu

Tiberiu Capudean is just old enough to remember the end of communism in his home country of Romania, in Eastern Europe. Romania had a particularly oppressive communist dictator before its revolution in 1989. Romanian society was strictly regulated, and the danger in not conforming was very high. People who questioned the government often "disappeared" and never returned. Post-communism, the Romanian Orthodox Church has a massive amount of power with deep ties in government—it's also extremely anti-LGBTQ.

As an adult, Tiberiu has had a chance to travel abroad and see what the LGBTQ community looks like in other places, and he sees his country becoming comparable sometime in the future. "In Spain for instance or UK, France, there is such a healthy gay culture in my opinion. People are free. This comes after decades of oppression and then decades of fighting, and probably [Romania will] be here like this in 50 years. . . . For so many years, people were hiding, and they were scared to be arrested if they were reported by neighbors or other people. For so many, for decades, they were not even dreaming of having a partner."

Today, Romania has a small LGBTQ community, with politically active organizations, a small pride parade and festival every year, and only a handful of gay businesses in the country. Romania also has the second highest rate of emigration in the world (following Syria), which means that a lot of LGBTQ people end up leaving the country to live in other places instead of staying to make changes at home.

Europe should not be assumed to have one attitude about LGBTQ people across all countries.

that are less open to LGBTQ people. Legalization of homosexuality is a mandatory condition to join the European Union. Tiberiu's home country, Romania, for example, only legalized homosexuality specifically because it was trying to join the EU; in fact, some people within the government were so opposed to the idea that they almost derailed the whole process. The EU also actively supports LGBTQ organizations throughout the region.

TEXT-DEPENDENT QUESTIONS

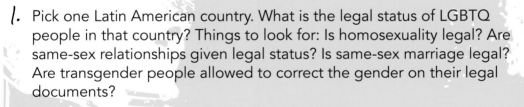

1. What is a "two-spirit" person, according to Native American tradition?

2. Which religion influenced the Latin American perspective on LGBTQ people?

3. What type of government shaped the Eastern European perspective on LGBTQ people?

4. How does the European Union help LGBTQ people?

RESEARCH PROJECTS

1. Pick one Latin American country. What is the legal status of LGBTQ people in that country? Things to look for: Is homosexuality legal? Are same-sex relationships given legal status? Is same-sex marriage legal? Are transgender people allowed to correct the gender on their legal documents?

2. Pick one European country. What is the legal status of LGBTQ people in that country? Things to look for: Is homosexuality legal? Are same-sex relationships given legal status? Is same-sex marriage legal? Are transgender people allowed to correct the gender on their legal documents?

2

MIDDLE EAST AND AFRICA

WORDS TO UNDERSTAND

CULTURAL IMPERIALISM: *The idea that forms of colonialism still exist in a subtler way, through cultural and political pressure instead of conquering and colonizing. Also called "neo-colonialism."*

PLURALISTIC: *A system in which multiple cultures or philosophies are allowed to coexist peacefully.*

SUB-SAHARAN: *The part of Africa that lies below the Sahara Desert.*

THEOCRACY: *A government controlled by a religion or religious leaders.*

The Middle East is one of the most difficult regions in the world for LGBTQ people. It is a place that can be extremely dangerous to those who are open about their sexual and gender identity.

Stories are common in the Middle East of people being arrested for being gay.

THE MIDDLE EAST

Sam (not his real name) grew up in Baghdad, Iraq, where he saw firsthand the dangers that being openly gay would bring. A neighborhood boy told Sam that he was going to talk to his family about his own sexual orientation. And then the boy disappeared. His body was found weeks later with signs of torture. "Honor killings" are tragically common in the Middle East and elsewhere. An honor killing is when people kill a member of their own family as a way of making up for a perceived loss of honor brought on by that family member. There are many reasons a family might do this, but LGBTQ people are especially at risk.

Sam was a teenager when the U.S. invasion of Iraq occurred. He worked with the U.S. Army as a translator; as a result, he and his

The laws of most of the countries in the Middle East impose extreme punishments for the crime of homosexuality.

family were threatened, forcing them to flee Iraq and go to Syria. While in his teens and early adulthood, he was able to find other LGBTQ people while working at a restaurant in Damascus. Sam had a gay friend at the restaurant. It took a while for them to come out to each other. They would hint and wait to see the other person's reaction and then hint a little more strongly, until they were finally able to talk about it openly. Through connections like this, Sam was able to meet others. "People would rent villas and throw parties,"

Much of the Middle East's attitudes toward LGBTQ people is shaped by the spread of conservative and fundamentalist Islamic beliefs.

sometimes with dozens of people attending, where they could be open among themselves. But a gray cloud of danger still hung over them. Stories of people being arrested were common. Sometimes the people came back. Sometimes they didn't.

A Dangerous Place for LGBTQ People

The laws of most of the countries in the Middle East explicitly forbid homosexuality and impose extreme punishments for those crimes. Most of the religious sects also forbid it in no uncertain terms, and the cultural attitudes also strongly oppose it. "There is no real community," Sam says.

Interestingly, some countries can be more open to transgender people. For example, even though it is an extremely strict **theocracy**, Iran allows gender-affirming surgery for transgender people. As the Human Rights Campaign explains on its Web site, "The basis for this attitude of acceptance is the belief that a person is born transgender but chooses to be homosexual, making homosexuality a sin."

Islam

Much of the Middle's East attitudes toward LGBTQ people is shaped by the spread of the religion Islam. Although there is no central authority within Islam to state an official doctrine for the religion, almost all interpretations exclude the possibility of acceptance for gay men and lesbians.

Much like Christianity in Europe, the Americas, and elsewhere, Islam spread largely through conquering societies and then forcing the religion upon them. The founder of Islam, Muhammed, lived in the 7th century in what today is Saudi Arabia. It was his successors over the next few decades who made the first major expansion of Muslim lands, though it was centuries before that Arab leaders forced the people of those areas to become Muslim.

Until then, the region had been a patchwork of local religions. Since the suppression of these traditions was so complete, it's difficult to know what their attitudes toward LGBTQ people were. Some that did survive the conquest, though, like Zoroastrianism (an ancient religion that existed in Iran before Islam and has survived to the present), are similarly opposed to homosexuality.

In Lebanon there are openly gay organizations and a nightlife unlike other countries of the Middle East.

A Couple Exceptions

Although the region as a whole is quite hostile to LGBTQ people, there are a couple areas that are a bit more open. Lebanon is considered to be comparatively LGBTQ-friendly. Although there is still significant opposition and a vague law that could be used against gay people, there are openly gay organizations and a nightlife unlike anything that can be found in most of the countries of the Middle East.

It seems likely that the Middle East will become more open to LGBTQ people.

Israel is another country in which LGBTQ people can be more open. Unlike the rest of the region, Israel is predominantly Jewish. Although there is a portion of Israeli society that is extremely conservative, it is more **pluralistic** in terms of cultural attitudes. As a consequence, LGBTQ people can be more open about their sexual and gender identity. Tel Aviv, a beach city on the Mediterranean, is even a major gay tourist destination.

The Future

Although extremely small now, there is a minority opinion within Islam that is becoming more open to LGBTQ people. This is most evident in Lebanon and in parts of the West. It seems likely that, like in other places in the world, the Middle East will become more open to LGBTQ people as more information is available and as more people realize that sexual minorities live among them. The Iranian president once proclaimed that there were no gay people in Iran; as it becomes more obvious that this is false, other arguments against LGBTQ people will fall away as well.

AFRICA

Africa is broadly divided into North Africa and **sub-Saharan** Africa, referring to anything below the Sahara Desert. The desert is so barren and uninhabitable that for much of history, it served as a natural barrier between the two regions, making them very different in terms of culture, ethnicity, and religion, because cultural interaction was much more difficult.

The Mediterranean coast of North Africa was part of the Arab conquests that spread Islam through large portions of the world. The conquests even made it as far as what is now Spain! As a result, North Africa is, in many ways, closer to the culture of the Middle East than it is to the rest of Africa. Just like the Middle East, the area's attitudes toward LGBTQ people are shaped by the influence of Islam. Being a sexual or gender minority can be very dangerous in these countries, leading to both legal issues and violence.

North Africa is, in many ways, closer to the culture of the Middle East than it is to the rest of Africa.

Prior to Western colonization, there are no records of any African laws against homosexuality.

Before Colonization

Like in Latin America and some other parts of the world, Africa's history can be divided into pre- and post-European colonialism. In pre-colonial times, Africa had a collection of native empires and kingdoms that covered much of the continent, and elsewhere the structure was mostly ordered by clans and tribes. Although it's impossible to know the attitude of all of these ancient civilizations toward LGBTQ people, there is reason to think that some acceptance of sexual minorities did occur. As prominent gay rights advocate Peter Tatchell told the *Guardian* newspaper, "Prior to Western colonization, there are no records of any African laws against homosexuality."

Indeed, at least one group that had limited interaction with European influence accepted homosexuality as an important part of their culture. According to the *Guardian*, "Anthropologists found an ethnic group in central Africa where it was customary for a male warrior to marry a teenage boy."

European powers formed colonies along the coasts of Africa, particularly West Africa and the southern tip.

European Influence

During the same period of exploration that saw European powers begin to expand into the Americas, they began to form colonies along the coasts of Africa, particularly West Africa and the southern tip. It was during this period that the slave trade began, when European colonists started exporting Africans as commodities to work in the other parts of the world that they controlled. But it wasn't until the late 1800s that Europeans began to move further inland to find new areas to conquer. The "scramble for Africa," as it's called, eventually led to nearly all of Africa being divided among European countries. During that time, colonists enforced their oppressive, discriminatory laws upon the locals.

LGBTQ advocates on the African continent bravely continue to fight for visibility.

Sadly, many African leaders have taken hold of those laws so adamantly that they believe them to be traditionally African, even though they did not exist before European colonization. They even go so far as to say that by preserving anti-LGBTQ laws, they are fighting against the influence of the West, specifically Europe and North America.

As far as religion goes, although Islam has reached further into more parts of the continent than just North Africa, sub-Saharan Africa is more commonly Christian due to European influence. Some native religion has survived, but it is in the minority.

International organizations continue to encourage greater openness for LGBTQ people.

Present and Future

Unlike a lot of the world, Africa has become less tolerant of LGBTQ people over the last several years, according to Amnesty International, a human rights organization that operates all over the world. "Sex between adults of the same sex—often characterized as 'unnatural carnal acts' or 'acts against the order of nature'—is currently a crime in 31 countries in sub-Saharan Africa, as well as all of North Africa. In four countries in the region, it carries the death penalty." Believing that they are pushing back against **cultural imperialism**, many African countries are making laws that are even more severe than the colonial-era ones. Strangely, several countries have tightened their anti-LGBTQ laws partly in response to pressure by U.S.-based evangelical groups, embracing cultural influence from some Western sources, while saying that they are resisting outside influence.

Nigeria, the most populous country in Africa, has some of the most extreme laws on the continent—or in the world. Not only is homosexuality illegal throughout the country, requiring jail sentences for those found guilty, but in some areas, it carries the death penalty. In addition, Nigeria's laws make it illegal to be part of an organization that promotes homosexuality, effectively making anyone who supports an LGBTQ human rights group subject to imprisonment.

There is some room for optimism though. LGBTQ advocates on the continent bravely continue to fight for visibility. International organizations continue to encourage greater openness, and LGBTQ people continue to fight their criminal sentences in court.

Global Gay: The Next Frontier in Human Rights

JEAN-CLAUDE

In March of 2011, Jean-Claude Roger Mbede was arrested by the police in Cameroon for the crime of "homosexuality and attempted homosexuality," according to Amnesty International. The evidence against him consisted of one text message, in which he told a man "that he was in love with him." Eventually, "he was sentenced to three years' imprisonment. During his time in jail, he suffered from malnutrition and regular beatings. Although he was granted a provisional release on July 16, 2012, while his lawyer was appealing his case, the Yaoundé Court of Appeal then upheld his sentence. Fearing re-arrest and being forced to serve out the remainder of his sentence, Jean-Claude went into hiding." In January 2014, Jean-Claude passed away from a treatable condition because "his family prevented him from receiving necessary medical treatment." Sadly, his case is not unique. You can learn more about Jean-Claude in this chapter's educational video.

In many countries around the world homosexuality is a crime for which you can be arrested.

TEXT-DEPENDENT QUESTIONS

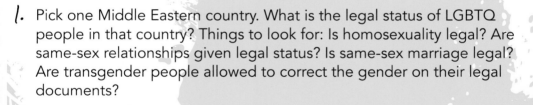

1. What is a theocracy? Can you give an example of one?

2. Name a country in the Middle East that is more accepting of LGBTQ people.

3. What was the "scramble for Africa"?

4. What is cultural imperialism?

RESEARCH PROJECTS

1. Pick one Middle Eastern country. What is the legal status of LGBTQ people in that country? Things to look for: Is homosexuality legal? Are same-sex relationships given legal status? Is same-sex marriage legal? Are transgender people allowed to correct the gender on their legal documents?

2. Pick one African country. What is the legal status of LGBTQ people in that country? Things to look for: Is homosexuality legal? Are same-sex relationships given legal status? Is same-sex marriage legal? Are transgender people allowed to correct the gender on their legal documents?

3

Asia and Oceania

WORDS TO UNDERSTAND

FA'AFAFINE: A Samoan person who does not conform to either gender role and is considered part of a "third gender."

GENDERQUEER: A person who blurs the line between genders and does not conform to the standard conception of how either gender should present itself.

HIJRA: A person who presents in the Indian tradition of gender non-conformity.

KATHOEY: A Thai person who could be referred to as a transgender woman, but who also includes feminine gay men and other genderqueer people; also called "ladyboys."

Ted Li grew up in a small town in northeast China in a region known as Inner Mongolia, disconnected from any LGBTQ community. "Similar to America, the smaller the city is, the more conservative people are," Ted says. "These days, for most gays in China, life is still pretty difficult, especially for those who live in third- or fourth-tier cities." After living in the United States as an exchange student in high school and then later as a college student, Ted returned to China and now lives in Beijing. "My life is comparatively easy compared to those gays living in small towns. But I came from a small town, so I can feel their pain and struggle. A lot of gays have to get married either to some lesbians or some women who have no idea of them being gays, due to tremendous pressure from their families, workplaces, and society."

But in larger cities, life is different. "Even if the majority of people still have misconceptions towards gay people, there are many people who could understand and love. These people are mostly young and well-educated. That's why I don't feel stressful here. I'm actually out to my coworkers . . . and some closest friends. But I'm not open to my dad or my stepmother. They are very conservative."

LGBTQ people generally have an easier time in big cities than in small towns.

As for Beijing, Ted says, "There are four or five gay bars in this huge city [21 million people], and on gay dating apps you could always see other gays around you even if most of them never use their own pictures in their profiles." It may not be as open as what he experienced while living in the United States but it's enough to have contact with other LGBTQ people.

ASIA: A WEALTH OF DIVERSITY

The continent of Asia is a vast area of land with a mind-boggling amount of cultural diversity. From the sub-continent of India in the south to China and Japan in the east and Malaysia in the southeast, the differences among cultures and peoples is in many ways greater than we find in other parts of the world.

Asia is also a more complicated religious landscape than much of the world. Islam spread through some portions of the region (including

The continent of Asia is a vast area of land with a mind-boggling amount of cultural diversity.

some places you might not expect, like the sizable Muslim minority in northwest China). India is the birthplace of more than one major world religion, including Hinduism, which is practiced in much of India, and Buddhism, which is now more common further east than in its country of origin. In addition to various forms of Buddhism, those Far East countries have their own homegrown sects, like Confucianism and Taoism in China, and Shintoism in Japan.

None of these religions has a single central authority to set doctrine (though some individual sects within the larger religion have leaders, like the Dalai Lama, who leads the Tibetan Buddhists), so there is no unified perspective on LGBTQ issues. Culturally, however, much of Asia leans to the conservative side in relation to sexual and gender minorities.

India has one of the richest LGBTQ histories in the world.

India

In September of 2018, the law against homosexuality that had survived from colonial times was finally struck down by the Indian Supreme Court. It had been 150 years since British colonists had imposed the law upon India. Much like other places in the world, India had internalized the perspective of its colonizers to a degree that it seemed like it had always been a part of its own culture.

But India has one of the richest LGBTQ histories in the world. There are many references to queer people in Hindu mythology.

Various gods have sex with members of their own gender. Mythological figures change gender or have no gender. Hindu temples have carvings depicting homosexual sex. One myth describes a woman who was raised as a man and given an arranged marriage to a woman. When the woman finds out and sends him away, a spirit grants his wish of becoming a man, and he returns to marry his fiancé.

It's not clear what caused the change in modern China's cultural attitudes toward LGBTQ people.

A group of people called the **hijra** serve a prominent role in Indian culture. As *Gay Star News* reports, the word *hijra* is often translated as *transgender*, but "it's a far more complicated social and cultural identity than that. While they are shunned in some circumstances, they are also important to Indian cultural life. No Hindu wedding is blessed if hijra don't attend it. And increasingly, they are getting protection and are starting to get access to better jobs." They are even now able to get government documents that identify them as "third gender."

Modern Indian culture is less accepting than its history might imply, but attitudes are changing, as the Supreme Court ruling on gay marriage shows.

China

Traditional Chinese culture was not hostile toward LGBTQ people. Stories of LGBTQ relationships are scattered throughout its thousands of

Traditional Chinese culture was not hostile toward LGBTQ people.

years of history. One famous example was the Emperor Ai, who woke up with his male lover, Dong Xian, asleep on the sleeve of his shirt. Instead of waking him by moving, Ai cut off his sleeve to get out of bed, while letting Dong Xian sleep. This led to the term *cut sleeve* being used as slang for homosexuality, a meaning it has kept to the present day.

As the *Economist* magazine explains, "In sharp contrast to Christianity and Islam, Chinese religious and social thinking does not harshly condemn same-sex relationships. Taoism regarded homosexual sex as neither good nor bad, while Confucianism, by encouraging close relations between master and pupils, is sometimes thought to have indirectly encouraged it. China's greatest novel, *The Dream of the Red Chamber*, written in the late 18th century, includes both heterosexual and same-sex relations."

It's not totally clear what caused the change in China's cultural attitudes toward LGBTQ people. Interaction with the West may have been a factor, as well as the cultural emphasis on family roles. One factor that is preventing change is China's communist government. As we saw in Eastern Europe, communism tends to be anti-LGBTQ because it emphasizes an individual's role within society at the expense of individualism. Also, in most of the world, change has been brought through civil society—advocacy organizations, protests, and information shared through the free media that are legally protected. The government very strictly controls civil society in China, making change very difficult. It's very telling that Taiwan, which has a shared history and culture with China, but a more democratic government, has much greater rights for LGBTQ people and even allows same-sex marriage.

Japanese Buddhist monks were well known to have sex among themselves.

Being Gay in Deeply Conservative China

Japan

Shintoism, the native religion of Japan, which began to form around 1000 BC, is silent on the subject of anything LGBTQ. Buddhism made its way to Japan much later but still didn't have anything negative to say about sexual or gender minorities. One of the interesting things about Buddhism is that it has been adapted many times in different cultural contexts. The Japanese form actually began to take on a prominent aspect of homosexuality, particularly among men. Buddhist monks were well known to have sex among themselves, and it wasn't considered a big deal.

Samurai were expected to enter into relationships between mentor and apprentice, relationships that were generally accepted to have a sexual element to them. We aren't necessarily talking about love here, though, since the mentoring relationship ended as the apprentice came into his own as a samurai. They were still expected to have a strong bond, but anything more had to be broken off.

Sexual relationships between monks and samurai were common enough that visiting Europeans during the Middle Ages were a bit surprised by them and wrote about them in their travelogues.

Although there is still no real religious objection to LGBTQ people in Japan, at some point Japanese culture became more conservative. Although Japan was never conquered by any European powers, it's still believed that interaction with the West affected attitudes toward sexual and gender minorities. But whether through Western influence or natural cultural evolution, Japan today is not completely open. While Japanese people generally don't need to worry about their safety or legal issues because of their sexual or gender identity, there can be very negative consequences to a person's social, family, and professional life.

Nevertheless, things are becoming more open in Japan. The LGBTQ community is becoming more visible. Tokyo has a famously thriving gay nightlife. And cultural attitudes are becoming more accepting of diversity.

Samurai were expected to enter into sexual relationships between mentor and apprentice.

Whole city blocks in places like Bangkok and Phuket are dedicated to the *kathoeys*.

Kathoeys in Thailand

Thailand is generally considered to be one of the more open and accepting countries in Asia. No laws forbid LGBTQ identities or activities. Bangkok, the capital, has a very visible gay nightlife, and LGBTQ people can be open in public, generally without fear of violence.

In fact, there is a very prominent and celebrated segment of society that fits under the queer umbrella. The word that is used to describe them, *kathoey*, is often translated as *transgender*. They are also often referred to as "ladyboys." But the way Thai people perceive *kathoeys* is more complicated. Some are indeed transgender women and many end up transitioning, a process that is legal in Thailand and relatively inexpensive and easy compared to many other parts of the world. But others are feminine-presenting gay men or what we would call "drag queens," meaning they dress as a woman as a performance or for fun. And still others consider themselves a "second type of woman" or what we would might call genderqueer.

Whole city blocks in places like Bangkok and Phuket are dedicated to the *kathoeys*. Bars that they frequent are popular destinations, and their cabaret shows are considered some of the things that tourists must experience when visiting Thailand.

Australia's and New Zealand's laws defend the rights of LGBTQ people.

OCEANIA

Australia and New Zealand

Australia and New Zealand have a strong cultural and political connection to Europe. Consequently, their cultural attitudes toward LGBTQ people are quite similar to those of Europe, making them arguably the most open in the region. Both countries legally protect LGBTQ people, and both allow same-sex marriage. The LGBTQ community looks similar to what you would find in Europe or North America, with gay organizations and businesses prevalent and accepted.

Samoan culture embraces individualism, and people are not expected to fill rigid positions in society.

FA'AFAFINES IN SAMOA

Translated directly, *Fa'afafine* means "in the manner of woman." This is often interpreted to mean transgender, but like the terms used for non-binary people in other cultures, the real meaning is slightly different. In the Pacific island nation of Samoa, to be a *fa'afafine* is considered to be part of a third gender.

Samoan culture embraces individualism. People are not expected to fill rigid positions in society. As a result, *fa'afafines* are allowed express themselves as they wish.

The Pacific Islands

The Pacific Islands are the many islands that dot the Pacific Ocean between Asia and the Americas. They include everything from Palau and Papua New Guinea in the west, to the Hawaiian islands in the northeast, to French Polynesia in the southeast. Many of the islands were colonized by European nations and experienced similar colonial rule to the other places that have been discussed. Although they are ethnically and culturally linked, it's impossible to make generalizations about Pacific Islander attitudes toward LGBTQ people, particularly before colonization. However, there are indications that LGBTQ people have had a role within some traditional cultures. For an example within the Samoan culture, see the sidebar about *fa'afafines*.

The Pacific Islands encompass the
many islands that dot the Pacific Ocean
between Asia and the Americas.

TEXT-DEPENDENT QUESTIONS

1. What did Indian's Supreme Court rule recently regarding same-sex marriage?

2. What is a *kathoey*?

3. What is a *fa'afafine*?

RESEARCH PROJECTS

1. Pick one Asian country. What is the legal status of LGBTQ people in that country? Things to look for: Is homosexuality legal? Are same-sex relationships given legal status? Is same-sex marriage legal? Are transgender people allowed to correct the gender on their legal documents?

2. Pick one Pacific Island nation. What is the legal status of LGBTQ people in that country? Things to look for: Is homosexuality legal? Are same-sex relationships given legal status? Is same-sex marriage legal? Are transgender people allowed to correct the gender on their legal documents?

4

International LGBTQ Issues

WORDS TO UNDERSTAND

ASYLUM: When a country provides protection for a person who is facing danger in their own country.

INTER-GOVERNMENTAL ORGANIZATIONS (IGOs): An international organization that coordinates the work of individual countries' governments.

NON-GOVERNMENTAL ORGANIZATIONS (NGOs): A transnational organization that works across borders without having formal ties with any particular nation's government.

REFUGEE: A person who has fled their own country because of danger, war, or disaster.

Despite the great diversity within the global LGBTQ community, some common issues do cross borders.

The United Nations has created programs to promote equal rights for LGBTQ people across the globe.

Despite the great diversity within the global LGBTQ community, and despite the extremely varied conditions for LGBTQ throughout the world, some common issues—and the international organizations that seek to confront them—do cross borders. Very few issues are solely local in the 21st century, and activism is learning to adapt to that reality.

There are quite a few organizations that work internationally to promote LGBTQ rights. These organizations can be divided into two types: NGOs and IGOs. **Intergovernmental organizations (IGOs)** are groups that involve the governments of the countries themselves coordinating work. **Non-governmental organizations (NGOs)** are groups that work across borders but do not directly involve any country's government.

The United Nations is the biggest example of an IGO in the world; coordination among all of the governments of the world is its entire purpose. Among other important efforts, the UN has created the UN Free and Equal Program, which, according to its Web site, is "an unprecedented global UN public information campaign aimed at promoting equal rights and fair treatment of LGBTI people. In 2017, UN Free and Equal reached 2.4 billion social media feeds around the world and generated a stream of widely shared materials."

Human Rights Watch is a watchdog group that monitors LGBTQ rights abuses around the world.

The International Lesbian, Gay, Trans, and Intersex Association (ILGA) is an NGO that serves as a network of rights organizations—both national and local—all over the world. They advocate at the international level, including at the United Nations. According to their Web site, they also "support our members and other organizations in promoting and protecting human rights" and "raise awareness and inform institutions, government, media and civil society through advocacy and research."

Human Rights Watch is a watchdog group that monitors rights abuses around the world. According to hrw.org, "Human Rights Watch works for lesbian, gay, bisexual, and transgender peoples' rights, and with activists representing a multiplicity of identities and issues. We document and expose abuses based on sexual orientation and gender identity worldwide, including torture, killing and executions, arrests under unjust laws, unequal treatment, censorship, medical abuses, discrimination in health and jobs and housing, domestic violence, abuses against children, and denial of family rights and recognition.

Amnesty International: "We investigate and expose the facts, whenever and wherever abuses happen."

We advocate for laws and policies that will protect everyone's dignity. We work for a world where all people can enjoy their rights fully."

Amnesty International is another NGO that serves as a watchdog and advocacy group. On their Web site, they provide their mission statement: "We investigate and expose the facts, whenever and wherever abuses happen. We lobby governments, and other powerful groups such as companies. Making sure they keep their promises and respect international law. By telling the powerful stories of the people we work with, we mobilize millions of supporters around the world to campaign for change and to stand in defense of activists on the frontline. We support people to claim their rights through education and training."

These are only a few of the many organizations that work around the world to fight for LGBTQ rights.

The plight of LGBTQ refugees is an international issue.

REFUGEES

One international issue that has received more attention in recent years is the plight of LGBTQ **refugees**. Remember Sam from Iraq in Chapter 2? Because he worked with the U.S. Army as an interpreter in Iraq and had to flee from his home country as a result, he was given the chance to obtain **asylum** in the United States. In order to apply for refugee status, a person must have fled from their home country and be living in a second country. A refugee, by definition, is a displaced person. Sam was required to apply through the United Nations while living in Syria. While he was going through the application process, he didn't know where he was going to end up, but once he was approved, he found out that the United States had accepted his particular case. Altogether, the process took about two years from the first application to flying to the United States which is a shorter process than most people go through. Sam arrived in Houston, Texas, in 2009. Although his refugee status had more to do with his interpreter work than his sexual orientation, he was later able to sponsor the asylum application of a gay friend from Syria who had fled his home country as well, out of fear for his life because of his sexuality.

Sam and his friend are not alone. LGBTQ people from around the world—anywhere that they are in danger—are eligible to apply for refugee status. LGBTQ people seeking asylum come from places as diverse as African countries, Russia, and China.

Even for refugees like Sam, who are not applying based upon their sexual orientation but are refugees for other reasons, LGBTQ people face unique problems once they are resettled. As the U.S. Department of State points out on its Web site, "LGBT refugees may flee their countries due to persecution based on their sexual orientation or gender identity, or for the same reasons as any other refugee—such

ARRIVAL IMMIGRATION

Automated Lanes
Singaporeans, Permanent Residents & Long Term Pass Holders

LGBTQ people from around the world are eligible to apply for refugee status in the United States.

All refugees face significant challenges when arriving in a new country.

as ethnic conflict, political unrest, or the lack of religious freedom. However, in countries where they seek safety, LGBT refugees often risk being harassed, hurt, or even killed. They may be targeted by other refugees, host communities, or government officials and police, who may threaten to arrest and detain them."

After arriving in the United States, Sam worked as an interpreter for the local refugee agency to help them with new arrivals. But when word got out about his personal life, he found that some of the refugees didn't want him to be their interpreter anymore. Refugees are sometimes stuck between two worlds. Where they came from is still part of them, as they struggle to adjust to their new home.

All refugees face significant challenges when arriving in a new country. Once relocated, refugees in the United States are given about four months' worth of support before being expected to support

KISS ME!

Kissing does not give you HIV.

(But you don't want to, do you?)

—Tyler

キスミー！

キスではHIVは感染りません

（でも正直、俺とはしたくないよね）

—Tyler

themselves. For someone coming to a new country, sometimes with limited language skills, and almost always immediately after facing some extreme trauma, this can be a very difficult transition. It's extremely common for refugees to suffer from post-traumatic stress disorder (PTSD), a mental health condition in which people experience extreme anxiety, depression, and/or other emotional distress. For LGBTQ people, all of this often must be faced without the help or support of family.

The World Health Organization is a major leader in global AIDS treatment and prevention efforts.

HIV AND AIDS

In the early 1980s, a virus was discovered that is now known as the human immunodeficiency virus (HIV). This virus causes a condition known as AIDS (acquired immunodeficiency syndrome). In brief, HIV (the virus) weakens a person's immune system to such a degree that it becomes vulnerable to many types of diseases that our bodies normally fight off easily. That condition of vulnerability is what is known as AIDS. HIV is usually transmitted through bodily fluids, generally through sex, a blood transfusion, or sharing of hypodermic needles. Since the beginning, LGBTQ people have been especially hard-hit by HIV and AIDS, particularly gay men and trans women, making it one of the biggest challenges that the international LBGTQ community has to face.

Despite its horrors, the epidemic has at times brought out the best in the LGBTQ community, bringing people together to fight against a great threat to the life of the community. For decades, LGBTQ people and their allies have created organizations to advocate for those who suffer from the disease and to prevent its continued spreading. As time went on, governments became involved as well, and as the disease went global, so did the scope of the organizations. Although LGBTQ people are not the only ones affected by HIV/AIDS, they are especially at risk and are consequently a special focus in international efforts to end the disease.

Advocacy groups have been focusing on making sure that HIV/AIDS treatment is available to people all over the world.

There are both NGOs and IGOs working to fight HIV/AIDS. One of the most influential IGOs is the United Nations, whose UNAIDS department takes the lead in coordinating international HIV/AIDS work. The World Health Organization is also a major leader in global treatment and prevention efforts. There are also a large number of non-profit NGOs that work on treating and preventing the spread of HIV/AIDS. One example of this would be the Bill and Melinda Gates Foundation, which does a lot of work on HIV/AIDS, particularly in Africa.

Much progress is being made toward ending the epidemic, and these international organizations are leading the way. Since it has been discovered that those who are being treated for their HIV are much less likely to transmit the virus to others, advocacy groups have been focusing on making sure that treatment is available to people all over the world. Unfortunately, countries that make being openly gay or trans difficult or impossible also make the job of helping them receive treatment and prevent exposure extremely tough.

Much progress is being made toward ending the epidemic, and these international organizations are leading the way.

TEXT-DEPENDENT QUESTIONS

1. What is the difference between an IGO and an NGO?

2. What is the typical process for a refugee to gain asylum?

3. What countries or regions of the world do LGBTQ refugees come from?

RESEARCH PROJECT

Do a search online for an IGO or NGO that is not mentioned in this chapter that works on international LGBTQ issues. What type of work does it do? What need does it attempt to fulfill?

5

INTERNATIONAL RELATIONS

WORDS TO UNDERSTAND

CISGENDER: Someone who is not transgender; in other words, someone who identifies with the gender they were assigned at birth.

SEXUAL ORIENTATION OR GENDER IDENTITY (SOGI): Another way of referring to LGBTQ identities.

TRANSNATIONALISM: Something that extends across borders; in an LGBTQ context, a common transnational identity linking people across borders.

If you've read this far in this book, you probably have a strong interest in what life is like for LGBTQ people around the world. If you really want to explore the full range of experience and cultural diversity, the best way is to have personal interaction with people from other parts of the planet. Fortunately, there are many ways to go about doing this.

For those who are not able to travel, one of the best ways to make connections is through social media. You can search for Facebook groups that are specific to LGBTQ people in any particular

If you really want to explore cultural diversity, the best way is to meet people from other parts of the planet.

place you might be interested in. You'll be surprised at how often people will be interested in sharing their story with someone, even a stranger. Sometimes all you have to do is ask.

Another option for international interaction you may have in your area is getting involved by volunteering at a local refugee resettlement agency, which is an organization that assists refugees as they make their transition to living in their new country. You can check to see whether there is an agency near you at www.wrapsnet.org. You can also check to see whether your local LGBTQ organizations have any involvement with international issues or organizations. ILGA (International Lesbian, Gay, Bisexual, Trans, and Intersex Association) also has volunteering opportunities, which you can learn more about at https://ilga.org/volunteer. There are also likely immigrant communities in your area that you can reach out to in different ways. Sometimes just befriending a person from another country can be a great way to gain insight into another culture and other types of experience. If you are part of an immigrant community yourself, asking relatives and community members questions about their understanding of the LGBTQ people within their country of origin can be a great way to learn about others and connect with your own heritage.

There are likely immigrant communities in your area that you can reach out to.

TRAVEL

Perhaps the best way to open your mind to the great diversity of LGBTQ experience in the world is through travel. Nothing teaches you about a place better than being there, walking among the people, and talking with the LGBTQ people there about their lives and experiences.

There are different types of travel. Usually when we think about travel, we think about going on vacation somewhere as a tourist. While this is still a great experience to have, you may want to consider a broader type of travel. Just visiting the major tourist spots isn't really going to give you an idea of what a local culture is really like. It won't help you understand their lives. If you're able to get into a situation where you can have true cultural interaction, you'll be amazed at what a deeply profound experience it can be.

If you want to make long-term international travel a possibility for you, you can talk to your school counselor about doing a foreign-exchange program. Another option would be to do research on the study-abroad programs available at the colleges you might attend. Many schools have options for students to study in many diverse locations throughout the world.

> Perhaps the best way to open your mind to the great diversity of LGBTQ experience in the world is through travel.

If you are able to travel abroad, it can still be a challenge to find people from the LGBTQ community.

INTERACTION WHILE TRAVELING

If you are able to find a way to travel abroad, it can still be a challenge to find people from the LGBTQ community, especially in places where they have to be more discreet. Always keep safety as your top priority. Don't do anything that could endanger you or the people you are seeking to talk to.

Doing some research ahead of time on Facebook groups for LGBTQ people in the place that you're traveling to could provide some connections. Some places will have community centers similar to those you can find in the United States where you can meet local LGBTQ people. You may also want to do some research on LGBTQ organizations in the area you're visiting. In areas where the community is smaller or more hidden, people in these organizations might be just as curious about you as you are about them. If your international travel takes place after you turn 18, LGBTQ social media apps can be a great way to meet people wherever you are, since they are usually based on finding people near your location. You just need to do some research on what the most popular social media platforms in that area are, as they can vary from place to place.

Of course, one major factor in your ability to interact with locals while traveling is a common language. In many parts of the world it's possible to find English speakers, particularly among younger people in larger cities. You can't take that for granted, though. In most places in the world, it's still a great advantage to speak the local language. So, if there's a part of the world that you find especially interesting, you may want to start learning that language now to prepare for travel later in life.

In many countries consensual same-sex sexual activity may be illegal.

TRAVELING WHILE TRANS

For transgender and gender-non-conforming people, travel can be especially challenging. Not only is cultural understanding often frustratingly low in many parts of the world, but the legal documents that are used for travel can confuse people in most places. Depending on where a person is in their transitioning process, the gender marker on their passport may be different from how they are presenting their gender. The picture could also look very different if it has not been changed recently.

SAFETY FOR LGBTQ PEOPLE WHILE TRAVELING

The U.S. Department of State Web site gives some advice for LGBTQ people who are traveling abroad:

- Remember, you are subject to the laws of the country where you travel. In many countries, consensual same-sex sexual activity, public gathering, or dissemination of pro-LGBTQ material may be illegal. Read the country information for your destination for more details.
- Be cautious of potentially risky situations.
- Watch out for entrapment campaigns. Police in some countries monitor Web sites, mobile apps, or meeting places, so be cautious connecting with the local community.
- Be wary of new-found 'friends.' Criminals may target or attempt to extort LGBTQ foreigners.
- Some resorts or LGBTQ neighborhoods can be quite segregated. Be aware attitudes in surrounding areas can be much less accepting.

You can also find information specific to each country on the Department of State Web site.

This is not to say that travel is always dangerous, and you definitely shouldn't let that prevent you from seeing the world. You just need to know everything you can about the country before you go. For example, if you're in the liberal Netherlands, feel free to walk down the street holding hands with your partner, but if you're in the conservative Morocco, you really shouldn't do that.

What LGBTQ Life Is Like Around the World

For transgender and gender-non-conforming people, travel can be especially challenging.

The International Gay and Lesbian Travel Association (IGLTA) advises, "To avoid delays with airport security, if possible, be sure that the name, gender and date of birth on your airline reservations match information displayed on your government-issued photo ID or passport, which you must present at the airport.

"Know the laws, policies and attitudes of your travel destination and also be prepared that you may be mis-identified because many people across the globe do not know the difference between gender identity, gender presentation and sexual orientation. Whether or not you identify as a specific **sexual orientation or gender identity (SOGI)** minority, you may be perceived as belonging to a particular SOGI category and be targeted based on perception."

Many of the problems of international travel for trans people are similar to the issues they face every day—they just get magnified. None of this is to say that trans people should not attempt international travel: it just means that you should be prepared for an extra level of difficulty.

Trans people traveling should be prepared for an extra level of difficulty.

TRANSNATIONALISM

When a group of people have a common identity or common cause across borders, it is called **transnationalism**. Transnationalism can mean something as simple as reading about what LGBTQ life is like somewhere else, or it could be something as big as an international organization that is fighting for LGBTQ rights everywhere in the world.

For LGBTQ people, sharing a transnational identity could be a good thing for many reasons. If a person feels a connection with other people across borders, it could create greater motivation to those living in more "open" societies to provide political and other types of assistance to those living in more "closed" societies. Another potential benefit of transnationalism is more psychological in nature. If a person who feels persecuted where they

When a group of people have a common identity or common cause across borders, it is called transnationalism.

In practice, transnationalism often means that white, cis-gender, gay American men are the ones deciding what queer life looks like.

are becomes aware of a gay community in other places, it may help them to understand their own situation. The psychological benefits of a feeling of community are huge.

But LGBTQ transnationalism can have unintended negative consequences, too. For one, the way people talk about it can be counterproductive. LGBTQ transnationalism is often accused of enforcing Western ideas about what being LGBTQ means upon the rest of the world. Often it means that white, **cisgender**, gay American men are the ones deciding what queer life looks like, which is not how it should be. The American conception of what sexual and gender identity mean came out of a specific cultural background that does not exist anywhere else. As mentioned in the introduction, LGBTQ should not be expected to look the same everywhere in every cultural context. A helpful transnationalism would be open to all of the many ways in which sexual and gender minorities express themselves.

Another unintended consequence of LGBTQ transnationalism is that governments can sometimes use it against their own people. In many places in the world, including some parts of Eastern Europe, Africa, and Asia, political leaders will use the fact that LGBTQ people have connections abroad, and that they have people advocating for them abroad, to argue that they are a symbol of foreign interference in their country. Acceptance of LGBT people is portrayed as cultural imperialism. Nationalist leaders attempt to pit homophobia against transnationalism, or transnationalism against cultural purity. They try to convince people that they can only be patriotic *or* accepting of sexual and gender minorities, but not both. In this way, the LGBTQ community becomes a pawn used for other political purposes, shoring up national support by stoking homophobia.

But does a transnational identity even exist in the LGBTQ community? To answer that, we need to answer a couple other questions: Does someone feel a connection to someone else just because they are both LGBTQ, even if they are not from the same country? And are people interested in what happens to LGBTQ people in other countries?

Sometimes it's the shared experience of being excluded from mainstream society that creates a common identity.

It's possible that people in different countries who have very different backgrounds can still feel like they have some shared experiences. As Tiberiu from Romania in Chapter 1 says, "I think we have a sense of belonging because we've been bullied and discriminated against so much that if you meet somebody else just like you, you already know this guy has been through a lot. So, you sympathize, you empathize. You just have so much in common even though you don't know each other. He cannot hold his partner's hand in public just like you can't, so you have things in common." Sometimes it's a common experience from being excluded from mainstream society that creates a common identity, wherever you are in the world.

POPULAR LGBTQ TRAVEL BLOGS

Believe it or not, for some people travel is a full-time job. There is a growing number of people who make a living writing about their travels online, and there are even a number of bloggers who specialize in giving travel information and advice to LGBTQ people. Although there are many more out there, here are a few favorite LGBTQ travel blogs:

Travels of Adam. https://travelsofadam.com. The Web site of Adam Groffman, one of the most popular and successful gay travel bloggers. He writes "hipster guides" to cities all over the world and provides LGBTQ information.

Dopes on the Road. www.dopesontheroad.com. The blog of Meg and Lindsay Cale, a lesbian couple who travel both within the United States and internationally.

Life Travelers Traveling Life. http://lifetravelerstravelinglife.com. The travel blog of Aaron Edwards, a transgender man, and his girlfriend, Emily.

The Nomadic Boys. https://nomadicboys.com. A gay couple, Stefan from Greece and Sebastien from France, travel the world and interact with the gay community as they go.

The Rainbow Route. www.therainbowroute.com. Canadian lesbian couple Jen and Laura.

Two Bad Tourists. www.twobadtourists.com. American gay couple Auston and David.

We live at a time when life for LGBTQ people in most of the world is getting better.

WHAT DOES THE FUTURE HOLD?

The world is getting smaller. Information technology like the Internet allows people to communicate with each other across the planet as easily as they can with someone next door. Transportation technology allows us to travel more than ever before, allowing us to interact in person with people from all over the world. Through interactions like this, people realize that they have much in common and that their futures are linked.

There is a growing number of people who make a living writing about their travels online.

Sometimes we work under the assumption that history leads in one direction, meaning that LGBTQ rights are destined to move forward across the planet. While that does seem to be the direction of progress for most of the world, it's not the case everywhere, and it can't be assumed that it will last forever. As mentioned, some countries (particularly in Africa) have taken significant steps backward for LGBTQ rights. And over the long arc of history, we see a number of back-and-forth swings on cultural attitudes toward LGBTQ people. We live at a time when life for LGBTQ people in most of the world is getting better, but we can't become complacent about that. We have to keep in mind that gaining rights for LGBTQ people has always been a struggle. It's only together, through an international or transnational movement, that the LGBTQ people of the world will be able to find acceptance and full human rights.

TEXT-DEPENDENT QUESTIONS

1. Define *transnationalism*.

2. What are the unique travel challenges for trans people?

3. What are some ways to stay safe while traveling?

RESEARCH PROJECTS

1. Look through some of the LGBTQ travel blogs listed above. What parts of the world do you think would be especially interesting to see and experience the LGBTQ community in? Why?

2. Write out your thoughts about transnationalism. Do you think that there is a common identity across borders? Do you think that people can feel a connection based upon being a sexual or gender minority?

Series Glossary Of Key Terms

Agender (or neutrois, gender neutral, or genderless): Referring to someone who has little or no personal connection with gender.

Ally: Someone who supports equal civil rights, gender equality, and LGBTQ social movements; advocates on behalf of others; and challenges fear and discrimination in all its forms.

Asexual: An adjective used to describe people who do not experience sexual attraction. A person can also be aromantic, meaning they do not experience romantic attraction.

Asexual, or ace: Referring to someone who experiences little or no sexual attraction, or who experiences attraction but doesn't feel the need to act it out sexually. Many people who are asexual still identify with a specific sexual orientation.

Bigender: Referring to someone who identifies with both male and female genders, or even a third gender.

Binary: The belief that such things as gender identity have only two distinct, opposite, and disconnected forms. For example, the belief that only male and female genders exist. As a rejection of this belief, many people embrace a non-binary gender identity. (See **Gender nonconforming.**)

Biphobia: Fear of bisexuals, often based on stereotypes, including inaccurate associations with infidelity, promiscuity, and transmission of sexually transmitted infections.

Bisexual, or bi: Someone who is attracted to those of their same gender as well as to those of a different gender (for example, a woman who is attracted to both women and men). Some people use the word bisexual as an umbrella term to describe individuals that are attracted to more than one gender. In this way, the term is closely related to pansexual, or omnisexual, meaning someone who is attracted to people of any gender identity.

Butch, or masc: Someone whose gender expression is masculine. *Butch* is sometimes used as a derogatory term for lesbians, but it can also be claimed as an affirmative identity label.

Cisgender, or cis: A person whose gender identity matches the gender they were assigned at birth.

Coming out: The process through which a person accepts their sexual orientation and/or gender identity as part of their overall identity. For many, this involves sharing that identity with others, which makes it more of a lifetime process rather than just a one-time experience.

Cross-dresser: While anyone may wear clothes associated with a different sex, the term is typically used to refer to men who occasionally wear clothes, makeup, and accessories that are culturally associated with women. Those men typically identify as heterosexual. This activity is a form of gender expression and not done for entertainment purposes. Cross-dressers do not wish to permanently change their sex or live full-time as women.

Drag: The act of presenting as a different gender, usually for the purpose of entertainment (i.e., drag kings and queens). Many people who do drag do not wish to present as a different gender all of the time.

Gay: Someone who is attracted to those of their same gender. This is often used as an umbrella term but is used more specifically to describe men who are attracted to men.

Gender affirmation surgery: Medical procedures that some individuals elect to undergo to change their physical appearance to resemble more closely the way they view their gender identity.

Gender expression: The external manifestations of gender, expressed through such things as names, pronouns, clothing, haircuts, behavior, voice, and body characteristics.

Gender identity: One's internal, deeply held sense of gender. Some people identify completely with the gender they were assigned at birth (usually male or female), while others may identify with only a part of that gender or not at all. Some people identify with another gender entirely. Unlike gender expression, gender identity is not visible to others.

Gender nonconforming: Referring to someone whose gender identity and/or gender expression does not conform to the cultural or social expectations of gender, particularly in relation to male or female. This can be an umbrella term for many identities, including, but not limited to:

> **Genderfluid:** Someone whose gender identity and/or expression varies over time.

> **Genderqueer (or third gender):** Someone whose gender identity and/or expression falls between or outside of male and female.

Heterosexual: An adjective used to describe people whose enduring physical, romantic, and/ or emotional attraction is to people of the opposite sex. Also **straight**.

Homophobia: Fear of people who are attracted to the same sex. *Intolerance, bias,* or *prejudice* are usually more accurate descriptions of antipathy toward LGBTQ people.

Intergender: Referring to someone whose identity is between genders and/or a combination of gender identities and expressions.

Intersectionality: The idea that multiple identities intersect to create a whole that is different from its distinct parts. To understand someone, it is important to acknowledge that each of their identities is important and inextricably linked with all of the others. These can include identities related to gender, race, socioeconomic status, ethnicity, nationality, sexual orientation, religion, age, mental and/or physical ability, and more.

Intersex: Referring to someone who, due to a variety of factors, has reproductive or sexual anatomy that does not seem to fit the typical definitions for the female or male sex. Some people who are intersex may identify with the gender assigned to them at birth, while many others do not.

Lesbian: A woman who is attracted to other women. Some lesbians prefer to identify as gay women.

LGBTQ: Acronym for lesbian, gay, bisexual, transgender, and queer or questioning.

Non-binary and/or genderqueer: Terms used by some people who experience their gender identity and/or gender expression as falling outside the categories of man and woman. They may define their gender as falling somewhere in between man and woman, or they may define it as wholly different from these terms.

Out: Referring to a person who self-identifies as LGBTQ in their personal, public, and/or professional lives.

Pangender: Referring to a person whose identity comprises all or many gender identities and expressions.

Pride: The celebration of LGBTQ identities and the global LGBTQ community's resistance against discrimination and violence. Pride events are celebrated in many countries around the world, usually during the month of June to commemorate the Stonewall Riots that began in New York City in June 1969, a pivotal moment in the modern LGBTQ movement.

Queer: An adjective used by some people, particularly younger people, whose sexual orientation is not exclusively heterosexual (e.g., queer person, queer woman). Typically, for those who identify as queer, the terms *lesbian, gay,* and *bisexual* are perceived to be too limiting and/or fraught with cultural connotations that they feel don't apply to them. Some people may use *queer,* or more commonly *genderqueer*, to describe their gender identity and/or gender expression (see **non-binary** and/or **genderqueer**). Once considered a pejorative term, *queer* has been reclaimed by some LGBT people to describe themselves; however, it is not a universally accepted term, even within the LGBT community. When Q is seen at the end of LGBT, it may mean *queer* or *questioning*.

Questioning: A time in many people's lives when they question or experiment with their gender expression, gender identity, and/or sexual orientation. This experience is unique to everyone; for some, it can last a lifetime or be repeated many times over the course of a lifetime.

Sex: At birth, infants are commonly assigned a sex. This is usually based on the appearance of their external anatomy and is often confused with gender. However, a person's sex is actually a combination of bodily characteristics including chromosomes, hormones, internal and external reproductive organs, and secondary sex characteristics. As a result, there are many more sexes than just the binary male and female, just as there are many more genders than just male and female.

Sex reassignment surgery: See **Gender affirmation surgery**.

Sexual orientation: A person's enduring physical, romantic, and/or emotional attraction to another person. Gender identity and sexual orientation are not the same. Transgender people may be straight, lesbian, gay, bisexual, or queer. For example, a person who transitions from male to female and is attracted solely to men would typically identify as a straight woman.

Straight, or heterosexual: A word to describe women who are attracted to men and men who are attracted to women. This is not exclusive to those who are cisgender. For example, transgender men may identify as straight because they are attracted to women.

They/Them/Their: One of many sets of gender-neutral singular pronouns in English that can be used as an alternative to he/him/his or she/her/hers. Usage of this particular set is becoming increasingly prevalent, particularly within the LGBTQ community.

Transgender: An umbrella term for people whose gender identity and/or gender expression differs from what is typically associated with the sex they were assigned at birth. People under the transgender umbrella may describe themselves using one or more of a wide variety of terms—including transgender. A transgender identity is not dependent upon physical appearance or medical procedures.

Transgender man: People who were assigned female at birth but identify and live as a man may use this term to describe themselves. They may shorten it to *trans man*. Some may also use *FTM*, an abbreviation for *female-to-male*. Some may prefer to simply be called *men*, without any modifier. It is best to ask which term a person prefers.

Transgender woman: People who were assigned male at birth but identify and live as a woman may use this term to describe themselves. They may shorten it to *trans woman*. Some may also use *MTF*, an abbreviation for *male-to-female*. Some may prefer to simply be called *female*, without any modifier.

Transition: Altering one's birth sex is not a one-step procedure; it is a complex process that occurs over a long period of time. Transition can include some or all of the following personal, medical, and legal steps: telling one's family, friends, and co-workers; using a different name and new pronouns; dressing differently; changing one's name and/or sex on legal documents; hormone therapy; and possibly (though not always) one or more types of surgery. The exact steps involved in transition vary from person to person.

Transsexual: Someone who has undergone, or wishes to undergo, gender affirmation surgery. This is an older term that originated in the medical and psychological communities. Although many transgender people do not identify as transsexual, some still prefer the term.

FURTHER READING & INTERNET RESOURCES

BOOKS

Epprecht, Marc. *Sexuality and Social Justice in Africa: Rethinking Homophobia and Forging Resistance (African Arguments)*. New York: Zed Books, 2013.

This book explores the African LGBTQ opposition from many perspectives, including the political responses of African leaders, religious opposition, historical factors, and local variations.

Law, Benjamin. *Gaysia: Adventures in the Queer East*. Berkeley, CA: Cleis Press, 2012.

An Australian son of Asian immigrants, Benjamin Law, travels extensively throughout Asia—everywhere from China to Japan to Bali to Malaysia and more—to explore the breadth of diversity of the LGBTQ community in an entertaining and amusing way.

Luongo, Michael T., ed. *Gay Travels in the Muslim World*. New York: Haworth Inc., 2007.

A collection of first-person essays compiled with a range of experiences in a range of Muslim countries, this book gives a good introduction to what life is like around the world for gay Muslims.

WEB SITES

Amnesty International. https://www.amnesty.org
Amnesty is one of the largest human rights organizations in the world. Its mission includes fighting for LGBTQ rights. Its Web site includes information about its efforts in many different countries and ways to get involved.

Human Rights Watch. https://www.hrw.org/
Human Rights Watch is a leading international organization that tracks human rights around the world. Its Web site includes information about many different types of human rights issues in different countries.

ILGA. https://ilga.org
The International Lesbian, Gay, Trans and Intersex Association is an international network of LGBTQ organizations. Its Web site includes a directory of organizations around the world and information about how you can get involved.

Rainbow Europe. https://rainbow-europe.org
Rainbow Europe is a Web site created by ILGA-Europe. It includes information about the legal status of LGBTQ people in each European country, including an interactive map.

Gay Star News. https://www.gaystarnews.com
A gay news Web site that includes international LGBTQ news.

Pride celebrations, such as this one in Tel Aviv, Israel, are held in cities around the world. If you are able to visit one, it is a wonderful opportunity to meet people and appreciate the great diversity of the worldwide LGBTQ community.

INDEX

A

acquired immune deficiency syndrome (AIDS), 69–71
activism, 20, 25
Africa, 30, 36–41, 66, 71, 85, 87–88
Ai (emperor), 50
American Court of Human Rights, 17
Amnesty International, 40, 64, 93
Asia, 44–55, 85
asylum, 61, 67–70
Australia, 55

B

Balkans, 24
Bangkok, 54
Belgium, 27
Bill and Melinda Gates Foundation, 71
Brazil, 19–20
Buddhism, 48–52

C

Cameroon, 41
Capudean, Tiberiu, 27, 86
Catholic Church, 16–18, 23–24
Chechnya, 25
China, 45–51, 66
Christianity, 10–11, 22–23, 34, 39, 50
Cold War, 24–25
colonialism, 10–12, 37–40, 48–49, 55–57
coming out, 6
communism, 24–25, 51
community, 8–9, 75–88
Confucianism, 48
Czech Republic, 24

D

Dalai Lama, 48
Denmark, 23
diversity, 8–11
Dong Xian, 50
Dream of the Red Chamber, The, 50

E

Eastern Europe, 24–26, 85
Eastern Orthodox Church, 24–25
El Salvador, 20
Europe, 9–11, 21–28, 37–39, 55
European Union, 26–28

F

Fa'afafine, 45, 57
Facebook, 75, 78
France, 21, 23, 27
Free and Equal Program, 63
French Polynesia, 57

G

Gay Star News, 49, 93
gender identity, 45, 75, 90–92
genderqueer, 45, 54
Germany, 27
Greece, 22

H

Hawaiian Islands, 57
health, 70–73
hijra, 45, 48–49
Hinduism, 48–49
history, 10–12, 18, 22
Homosexual Liberation Front, 18–19
honor killings, 32
human immunodeficiency virus (HIV), 69–71
Human Rights Watch, 16–17, 63–64, 93

I

India, 45, 48–49
indigenous peoples, 14–15
Inner Mongolia, 45
intergovernmental organizations, 61–65, 70–71
International Gay and Lesbian Travel Association (IGLTA), 81–82
International Lesbian, Gay, Bisexual, Trans, and Intersex Association (ILGA), 11–12, 63, 76, 93
Internet, 75, 86, 88
Iran, 34, 36
Iraq, 32
Islam, 24–25, 33–36, 46–48, 50
Israel, 35
It Gets Better Project, 6–7
Italy, 23

J

Japan, 46–47, 51–53

K

Kadyrov, Ramzan, 24–25
kathoey, 45, 54

L

"ladyboys," 45, 54
language, 79
Latin America, 15–20, 37
laws, 10–11, 27–28, 33, 36–42, 48, 54–55, 71, 79–82
Lebanon, 34–35
Lesbos, 22

M

Malaysia, 46–48
marriage, 6, 9, 16–17, 51, 55
Mbede, Jean-Claude Roger, 41
Mexico, 17–19
Middle East, 30–36
minorities, 9
Morocco, 80
Muhammed, 34

N

Napoleonic Code, 18
Native Americans, 15, 29
Netherlands, 23, 80
New York City, 9
New Zealand, 55
Nigeria, 41
non-governmental organizations, 61–65, 71
North Africa, 36–40
North America, 11
Norway, 23

O

Oceania, 44–45, 55–58

P

Pacific Islands, 57–58
Palau, 57
Papua New Guinea, 57
parades, 8–9
Peña, Aldo Alexander, 20
persecution, 63–68
Phuket, 54
Poland, 24
politics, 20, 25, 85
post-traumatic stress disorder (PTSD), 70

Pride, 8–9
progress, 11–12
Putin, Vladimir, 24–25

Q

QR Video
    Albania, 26
    China, 51
    human rights, 41
    LGBTQ life around the world, 80
    UN LGBT rights history, 66

R

Rainbow Europe, 93
refugees, 61, 66–70
religion, 22–27, 33–35, 39–41, 46–50, 52
Romania, 24, 26–27, 86
Romanian Orthodox Church, 26–27
Rome, 22
Russia, 24–25, 66

S

safety, 78, 80–82
Samoa, 45, 56–57
samurai, 52–53
San Francisco, 9
Sappho, 22
Saudi Arabia, 34
Serbia, 24
sexual identity, 90–92
Shintoism, 48, 52
Slovakia, 24
social media, 75, 78, 86
Soviet Union, 24–25
Spain, 23, 36
statistics, 6, 8, 11–12, 17
Stonewall Riots, 9
Sub-Saharan Africa, 36–40
Supreme Court
    India, 48–49
    Mexico, 19
    United States, 19
Sweden, 23
Syria, 32–33, 66

T

Taiwan, 51
Taoism, 48
Tatchell, Peter, 37
Tel Aviv, 35
Thailand, 45, 54
Tibet, 48
transnationalism, 74–75, 82–88
travel, 74–88
two-spirit, 15, 29

U

UNAIDS, 71
United Kingdom, 23
United Nations, 61–63, 68, 70–71

V

violence, 24–25, 32, 41, 63, 66–68

W

West Africa, 39
Western influence, 37–39, 52
World Health Organization, 70

Z

Zoroastrianism, 34

AUTHOR'S BIOGRAPHY

Jeremy Quist is a writer and California native. He conducted academic research on LGBTQ identity and community in Eastern Europe and wrote about his experiences at www.we2boys.com. He's lived throughout the Western United States and now splits his time between Northern California and the road.

CREDITS

COVER

(clockwise from top left) Dreamstime/Belish; iStock/BrasilNut1; iStock/FG Trade; iStock/Rawpixel;

INTERIOR

1, iStock/Heather Shimmin; 3, iStock/justhavealook; 13, iStock/Salzburg13; 14, shutterstock/theteamtall; 16, shutterstock/dmitry_islentev; 17, shutterstock/Celso Diniz; 18, shutterstock/Javier Garcia; 19, shutterstock/Cassianhabib; 20, shutterstock/Milosz Maslanka; 21, shutterstock/Fokke Baarssen; 22, shutterstock/mato; 23, shutterstock/posztos; 25, shutterstock/kokoju; 26, shutterstock/URTIMUD PRODUCTIONS; 27, shutterstock/Alexandros Michailidis; 28, shutterstock/J. Carneros; 30, iStock/aiqingwang; 31, istock/jedraszak; 32, shutterstock/Shawn Goldberg; 33, iStock/ozgurdonmaz; 34, shutterstock/FredChimelli; 35, shutterstock/ColorMaker; 36, iStock/hadynyah; 37, iStock/himarkly; 38, iStock/Andrea Willmore; 39, shutterstock/Timothy Hodgkinson; 40, shutterstock/elbud; 42, shutterstock/kittirat roekburi; 44, shutterstock/dinozzzaver; 46, iStock/Xiansheng Dai; 47, iStock/tottoto; 48, iStock/SoumenNath; 49, dreamstime/tonyv3112; 50, dreamstime/rico leffanta; 51, shutterstock/Travel Stock; 53, shutterstock/Attila JANDI; 54, iStock/TwilightShow; 55, iStock/kaszojad; 56, Dreamstime/Rico leffanta; 58, dreamstime/Sergey Uryadnikov; 60, iStock/renato boriaza; 61, shutterstock/Shawn Goldberg; 62, dreamstime/Sean Pavone; 63, shutterstock/Casimiro PT; 64, shutterstock/Ryan Rodrick Beiler; 65, dreamstime/Arienne Davey; 67, iStock/joyt; 68, shutterstock/Daniel M Ernst; 69, shutterstock/cdrin; 70, dreamstime/Mohammed Ahmed Soliman; 71, shutterstock/kim7; 72, iStock/suze777; 74, shutterstock/yesfoto; 75, iStock/kaetana_istock; 76, dreamstime/Stuart Monk; 77, iStock/ViewApart; 78, iStock/Drazen; 79, shutterstock/Michaelpuche; 81, dreamstime/Phuttaphat Tipsana; 82, shutterstock/PiercarloAbate; 83, iStock/placebo365; 84, iStock/Drazen; 85, istock/jedraszak; 87, iStock/Dean Shim; 88, shutterstock/Anna Tamila; 94, shutterstock